Angry Black Man

Angry Black Man

Zion Turner

Tampa, Florida

Angry Black Man

Published by Gatekeeper Press
7853 Gunn Hwy., Suite 209
Tampa, FL 33626
www.GatekeeperPress.com

ISBN (paperback): 9781662943942

Dedications

To my father, Jessie Turner, for teaching me that the pen will always be mightier than the sword.

Table of Contents

Intro

At twenty years old, I stopped playing college basketball, dropped out of school, converted a Ford Transit van into a camper, and traveled around the country learning about the African Diaspora as a way of counteracting the "angry black man" stereotype. After years of research, six months of travel, and countless amounts of personal experiences, I'd like to explain to you why black men are so angry.

The Chattel Slavery Era
17th–19th Centuries

European Merchant

Up you go
My cargo load
Be careful not to die

If you do
Here is the truth
My pockets will surely slide

The Ghanaian Traitor

Inspired by the Transatlantic Slave Trade
The white man came to Africa
With a deal I could not resist
He offered guns and ammunition
To help me rule with an iron fist

In return, I gave him a few of our people
So he could turn them into slaves
I wish I knew the mistakes I made
Giving my brothers and sisters to the devil
Heavy on my heart my mistakes lay

They crammed our people onto boats
Packed to the brim like sardines
There was no bathroom either
The smell was obscene

After 80 days they landed on the shores of America
This is where the breaking process began
Stripping away all that made them African
This is where black shame began

Massa said:

Your last name is no longer Lumumba
It's Williams and Jackson

English is your language
So learn it well or you will pay
And no more Yoruba or Vodun
Christianity is the way

I don't want to hear any back talk
Or else a whooping's on the way
You're just a dumb black heathen
You're meant to be a slave

You eat when I say so
And work until you collapse
And if you fail to obey my rules
You will feel my wrath

No one's coming to save you
Better make yourself at home

I'm sorry brothers and sisters
We've left you all alone

Stranded

Your fireworks keep me up at night
My genes relate it to the crack of your whip
I'm starting to think this nation
Isn't a good fit

Unrecognizable to my motherland
They tell me how I've changed
My mind has been jumbled
Identity rearranged

I guess that makes me a slave
In this land I cannot escape
I'm going back to work now
Stranded, is my fate

A Day in the Life of a Chattel Slave

Inspired by Slavery in the US

The fresh lashes on my back have left me tossing and turning all night; I doubt I got a minute over an hour's worth of sleep. The only light to be seen is from the glow of a full moon, but massa's clock reads 4 am which means it's time to go to work. After a brief moment of silence and a yawn, I bear the weight of my fatigued body and float off into the crisp, dew-filled air and get to pickin'. The sun begins its steady ascent into the heavens when I accidentally cut myself on a thorn. "Ouch!" Back to work I go. After five hours of picking and cutting, picking and cutting, my blood-stained hands grip the rumble in my belly and blurry shapes begin to appear in the distance. I'm shaken from my work-induced state of starvation with a plate of food; it's a half pound of pork and some cornmeal. Without a second thought, I lick my plate clean, and slowly but surely, I begin to come back to myself. I overhear the plantation doctors in the distance talking about a bad case of drapetomania running through the south. I guess it's a disease that makes slaves hate their masters and want to leave the plantation. To me, drapetomania sounds like sanity, but I wouldn't dare tell massa that.

The doctors went on to say us slaves should be appreciative of the way we're treated around here, and that any sane slave would want to stay and work for the rest of their lives without any word of complaint. I'm not sure why he would say such a thing while tending to slaves dying of malnutrition and whuppin' wounds; I guess white folks just have a particular way of viewing things. A few more hours of picking go by and I'm able to find the courage to abandon my station in search of water. In the middle of my pursuit, I'm confronted by massa's daughter; she instructs me to tidy up the inside of the cabins. At least that's what I assume she said, her three-year-old grammar isn't always clear. Nonetheless, the message was received, so I redirect my attention towards the cabins about a half mile up the road. After the brief hike, I reach my destination, and to my surprise, a full water pail greets me on the front porch of the first cabin I am to clean. I gulp down so much water that I begin to feel a little nauseous, but we don't take breaks on this plantation, so I get to cleaning. I feel the water sloshing around in my belly with every move I make, and after a few short minutes, the sensation becomes unbearable. Instinctively, I round my back and puke up a gallon of water all over the floor. So here I am, knees and wrists deep in my own stomach acid, and somehow, I'm still thirsty. A tear starts to crawl down my cheek when, all of a sudden, the overseer comes bursting through the door, and lucky for me, his face reeks of lust and brandy. I reluctantly wipe the tear from my puffy cheek and turn on my back. After fighting this long and hard, I've learned it goes by quicker when I submit. He takes a long, sloppy minute to undo his belt but wastes no time imposing his will on me. Back and forth. Back and forth. I drift away to the days I was in my momma's arms swinging back and forth. This time I can't help but open up the floodgates, but before he gets the chance to see me cry, I thrust the knife from my back pocket into the side of his neck. I think I caught a case of drapetomania.

Radical Empathy

Before you judge
I need you to *see*
The pain that lives inside of *me*

You're scared to look
'Cause then you'll *see*
And make the same "mistake" as *me*

And pay the price of freedom
Whatever the cost may *be*
I dare you to see yourself in *me*

Post Traumatic Slave Disorder

America, you don't get it
You don't understand
I feel all the pain my ancestors endured on this land

My ears ring
With the cries of my daughter at the auction block
Torn away from my arms
Knowing she's destined for a life of sexual harm

Yeah I said it
I hope my words cause you harm
It's time to see the price behind the jewelry and charms

My lips tremble
As I speak these anti-American words
Jitter-pumped to the brim with adrenaline and spit
Blabbering away as I take another lash of the whip
For standing up to your tyranny

My back is strong as an ox
Yet under your control it breaks daily
Built up again by the God you praise daily

God talks to me too
And licks all my wounds
Preparing me for the day when your time is past due

Until then I will wait
Make no mistake
I am a man who embraces love
And hate

But my heart
Oh my great brass ticker
Shielding me from just enough pain
To make my skin thicker

This callous on my soul allows me to dig deep
And climb upward on this mountain of progress
No matter how steep

Kumbaya No More

Anger is the language of those
Whose cries are in vain
A last resort of the desperate
"You will feel my pain"

The Black Patriot

Inspired by the Life of Nat Turner

Ever since we stepped foot on this land
We were willing to fight
And lay down our lives to protect what's right

Whether it be a slave rebellion
Or fighting in the Civil War
America got more black patriots than she bargained for

Because a true patriot's goal is to protect the nation
From anyone who is unjust
Like slave masters and Confederate leaders
Who look at minorities with disgust

Stick around for the story of Nat Turner
And you will see
There's nothing more patriotic
Then paying the ultimate price to be free

Nat was born at the turn of the century
1800 to be exact
In a time where great evil was being done
That my friend is a fact

To witness dehumanizing abuse
Was an everyday occurrence

Which planted a seed of rebellion within Nat
That would eventually grow into insurgence

In the meantime Nat would get by
Doing normal slave things
Along with preaching from the Bible
About the change Moses would bring

He was a deeply religious man
With dedication and wit
And way too much intellect
To be controlled by a whip

This was proven at the age of twenty-one
When he escaped from the plantation
And survived in the woods all alone

But God came forth
Saying he escaped for selfish reasons
And told him to go back home

He obeyed at once
And was forced to confront
The evils of slavery once more

This time his rebellious seed
Grew twice the size

And shook Nat to the core

What is Nat to do
When the gatekeepers of his freedom
Refuse to loosen their grip?

What is Nat to do
When any talk of equality
Lands him ten lashes from the whip?

He must rebel
He must resist
He must bring change with his mighty black fist

So he preached by the fire
To those whose desire
To be free outweighed certain death

And they went on a mission
To fulfill a vision
Of freedom for blacks in the West

When the signal came
It was clear as an eclipse
In fact that's what it was

The very next summer

Nat and his soldiers took action
In the name of freedom, retribution, and love

Over the course of the night and into the day
Fifty-five white lives would be taken away
And for these souls I pray

Violence is never the first option
Second, third, fourth, or fifth
It's an option selected out of desperation
No one wants to be controlled by a whip

Nat knew this then
As well as I do now
But we can't be quick to scrutinize

We should be honest with ourselves
And acknowledge the truth
We've never felt the pain within their cries

So yes
Nat took away life and would soon pay the price
Two months later in a town called Jerusalem

He was interviewed by a reporter
In the gallows of prison
But he noticed Nat Turner's spirits had risen

He asked Nat
If he regretted his choice to rebel
Now that he was caught and soon to die

Nat looked him up and down
With a melancholy frown
And said:

Was not Christ Crucified?

Now I Get Why They Call It

Strange fruit
You see that?
It has boots

Swing Low Mother Africa

Rock me to sleep, Mother Africa. Wash away my impurities and fill the empty space with your unconditional love. Cradle my body in your tall, sweet grass while my mind melts away from this place. Take me further and further along until I land upon the shores of unity and grace, all with the help of your songbird's hypnotic tune. Teach me to love again. This world is a spawning ground of hate, and for my own sake, I'm learning to make peace with it. But even then I will not stand by and let manifest destiny ruin you again. So heal me, Mother Africa; lick the wounds I've acquired in this war that has no end. Stitch me up from head to toe with your blissful fortitude and empower me once more to face the shadows in the valley. I've been fighting this battle all my life, and I'm not sure how much more I have to give, but believe me when I tell you, I will lay down my life fighting for your preservation. For I know all too well that when the mother suffers, we all suffer. It may be fatigue talking, but I feel powerless against this opposing force. Their destructive ambitions have no limits, their blood lust is insatiable, and greed has tainted their hearts. Even so, your signal of distress will not be in vain. So sing your song just one more time, Mother Africa, the one that swings real low. Because, right now, I'm sinking, but your chariot can bring me home.

The Reconstruction and Jim Crow Eras
19th–20th Centuries

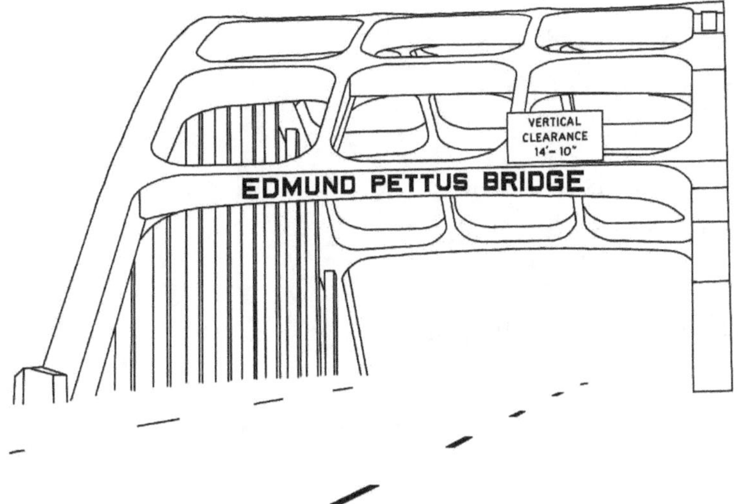

Frederick Says,

We fought in the war
Among "civil" nations
To bring liberation
Of the great black nation

The North won!
And now we are free
Free to beg, free to starve
Free to a life of poverty

They promised a mile
And only gave an inch
I can't say I'm surprised
We're caught in this pinch

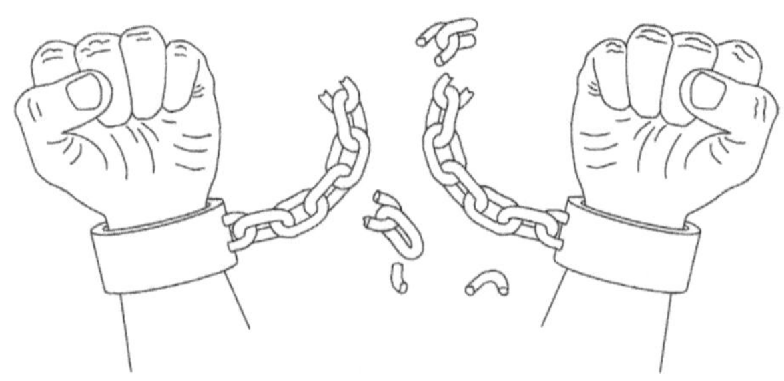

Neo Slavery

Inspired by the Reconstruction Era
Allow me to explain
How the chains have rearranged
Through the years to keep slavery alive

The 13th Amendment back in the day
Said it was illegal to be a slave
Except for the punishment of a crime

So they installed the black codes
And locked us up for petty crimes
Like staying out past curfew
Or talking out of line

The shackles were replaced
With a ball and chain and they erased
Any hope we would ever be free

So now I'm serving 1–3
In this land of liberty
On the chain gang working for free

My peers don't have it much better
They work the same exact shift
For pennies on the rich man's dollar
Pickin' the same cotton we did as slaves
Except now we're called sharecroppers

We make just enough cash to get by
Not enough to rise above
It's as if we're meant to be at the bottom
We fit like a glove

Not to mention we can't vote
But I think you understand
We're in the same old predicament
Enslaved on our captor's land

Em-Ploy-Ee

Em - meaning to put into
The opposite of me
I wonder what it means
To be an employee?

Ploy - meaning a cunning plan to capitalize
What do you mean?
This nation is so great
They wouldn't do this to me

Ee - meaning the recipient of said action
This is when I see
This system was created on my downfall
A slave is now an employee

The Great Migration

Inspired by the East St. Louis Race Riot

We left our homes in search of a life
More equal than the South would allow
The agony of a slave identity
Has brought our heads to a bow

So we followed the North Star
To a land far away
We hoped and prayed
It would save us one day

Some went to Chicago
Others to New York
And some went to East St. Louis
In search of good work

Upon arrival
We met familiar rivals
White supremacy was playing its sick little game

This time with a northern spin
The lesson would soon begin
There's no place for blacks to truly win

Nonetheless we were given jobs as promised
And better wages too

But the tension was boiling between us
And European immigrant groups

The Europeans refused to work
Until they got a higher wage
So we took their jobs and were happy with the pay
'Cause we were used to being slaves

The factories that employed us
Knew what they were doing
And wanted to break the strike

But trouble was brewing
And racist vows were renewing
Under the cover of a murky Missouri night

On the streets there were fights
Between blacks and whites
Over who could work the 9–5

On the 1st of July
The first bullets would fly
Out of a gun gripped by a white fist

That Ford Model T was disguised
In a black and white suit and tie
And performed what we call a drive-by

So we retaliated to protect our American Dream
The next car that came through
Was met with bullets and war screams

Two police officers were shot and killed
It sure was a scene
So much for our American Dream

The whites came in large numbers
With murder on their mind
No man, woman, or child
Could escape them this time

They burned, looted, brutalized, and lynched
Over one hundred black people were caught in this pinch
And that's the problem with the North

Everywhere Is War

So many lives sacrificed
For this American Dream
Oh the souls that have been sold
Fighting for this team

I call out to man and woman
Something isn't right
Instead of teaching us to fly
They teach us how to fight

"Pick a side," they say to me
You were told this too
"Turn your weapons against those
Who don't agree with you"

The bricks of this nation
Are mortared in with war
So I ask you now
Whose dream are we fighting for?

School House Blues

Inspired by twentieth century Segregational Tactics
The difference between white and black
Is all within the mind
But when it comes to school districts
The difference is property lines

And because where you live
Is also where you go to school
America created a wicked
Segregational tool

They marked red lines
Around communities that are white
And wouldn't let you live there
If your skin color wasn't right

And because we made less money
Due to economic discrimination
The quality of our schools suffered
Resulting in an underfunded education

I wonder if the creators of this red line
Ever looked hard enough at the facts
To realize they got their fancy schools
From exploiting browns and blacks

They live in an illusion of superiority

Money and power is the aim
Meanwhile our inferiority prescription
Leaves us drowsy with guilt and shame
We can barely get through a lesson
Without someone crying out in pain

Was it the drugs?
Or did someone cut themselves
On that broken window we can't afford to repair?

Was it the window?
Or are you crying
Because you hate the texture of your hair?

Either way it's a distraction
That sets the class even further back
Now we'll have to wait until 7th grade
To learn how to add and subtract

The Price of Freedom

All we want is civil rights
And we're willing to fight
All we want is what's due
Despite the tone of our hue

We will have what is ours
We're not afraid of the scars
We will have our respect
And deserve nothing less

Are you willing to comply?
Or will we have to die?
So you can see for yourself
The price of freedom is too high

Dualistic Dilemma

Control is the most powerful tool on earth and is meant to be dispersed amongst the masses. Why? Because control corrupts. When too much control is in the hands of the few, the line between the wants of the individual and the needs of the community begins to fade. This leads to the exploitation of the human body and the degradation of the spirit. I sit here as a man who can only imagine the magnitude of the oppressive fire that burnt my ancestors; after all, I've only inherited the scars left behind. No matter how hard I try to feel the full extent of their pain, I can only touch an imaginary version of the truth, which is nothing in comparison to the real thing. Nonetheless, this imaginary fire still burnt me in the most undesirable way, and although this is not about me, this fire has lit my wick and turned me into a weapon aimed directly at anything that might cause this assault to happen again. But to tell you the truth, I'm not exactly sure where to aim. Should we take up arms and fight to the death or grab our work boots and cast a ballot in the name of steady progress? Should we isolate ourselves from mainstream society and heal as a people or open up our arms and pockets to outside sources of healing? Should we go back to Africa and build our promised land where it all started, or have we paid too heavy a price to leave this American dream behind? To be frank, I'm not sure if I side with Malcolm or Martin.

Malcolm Luther X Jr.

The voice of the divine has split itself in two
This duality of change is long overdue

One with fiery-red hair
A temper that's sure to flair
And a devout sensibility to Islam

The other remains steady and cool
Under the pressure of racial duel
Christianity is the path he chose

But both of these courageous men
Share one common goal
To smack racism right on the nose

One is an extremist in nonviolence
The other thinks self-defense is our saving grace
One believes in integration
The other feels seclusion is best for our race

Together they're a polarizing bunch
Yet I have a hunch
We need both to make freedom ring

Because while one hand builds, the other destroys
What a wonderful, beautiful thing

Malcolm's Stance

Inspired by the Work of Malcolm X

I'm done bearing witness
To lynch mobs having their way
All the while being told
To keep sweet, pray, and obey
Freedom will come another day

Because you would be a fool
To trust the devil to pay his dues
He's shown us time and time again
His only intention is to bruise

We must defend ourselves
From this devil of a man
And this is why, brothers and sisters
I have devised a plan

We must defend our right to be human
Even if it lands us in the cemetery
And commit to the advancement of our race
By any means necessary

Because I'm done being the victim
In this codependent equation
Waiting on the freedom bus to come
When it never plans on arriving at our station

36

We must pool our resources together
And create our own bus
And never be left in the cold again
Anything short of this is unjust

When the white man sees what we're doing
It'll make him want to holler
But we will rebuild black wall street
Dollar by dollar

This is the great black future
That I wish to see
But I'm afraid in this lifetime
I've made a deadly enemy

So as I ponder this vision
From high in the sky
I'm shaken back to earth
By a gunshot cry

I guess this is goodbye

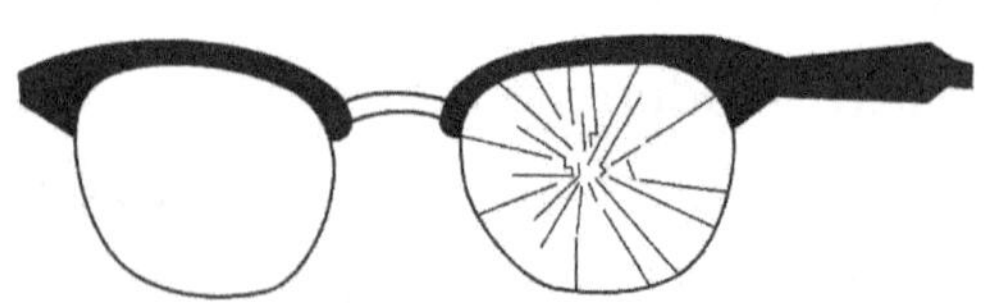

The White Black Man

Last night I had a vision
That war broke out
Between blacks and whites

But something was strange
That made my mind change
The leader of the blacks was white

His name was John Brown
And he fired a hundred rounds
Into the faces of slave masters and police

He laid down his life
To protect what's right
So his black brethren could be released

At this point I was confused
Morally bruised
And severely taken aback

But I learned not to see, but really look
Because sometimes I only see the cover
And not the contents of the book

Martin's Dream

Inspired by the Work of Dr. Martin Luther King Jr
I have a dream
That one day I won't have to dream anymore
And this land of injustice
Would forget about war

So the children's minds could stray
As they play the day away
Unafraid of stray bullets or slurs

I know it sounds crazy
But I was thinking just maybe
This is a life our children would prefer

But deep down I know
That you reap what you sow
And a hateful seed has been planted in your mind

You believe I am lesser
And yet the aggressor
In our human evolutionary line

All I ask of you now
As you sit and reflect
Is to see me as your equal
Not a suspect

Because I have a dream
Where that prejudicial weed has been picked
And the addiction to racism
Has long been kicked

Where a black woman dances
In the heat of the sun
Unafraid of a racist with a club, or gun

Where a white man walks
Through the thick of the hood
And isn't prejudged with owning a white one himself

This is the great future
That I wish to see
But I'm afraid in this lifetime
I've made a deadly enemy

So as I ponder this vision
From high in the sky
I'm shaken back to earth
By a gunshot cry

I guess this is goodbye

Deferred

In this world of illusionary things
It's hard to believe my words when I sing
Change gon' come, oh yes it will
It's just up there over that hill

I climb day and night
Fighting the good fight
I get to the top
Change nowhere in sight

They say there's one more hill to go
Just up the road
Don't they know
This game will make me explode?

The New Jim Crow
20th Century–Present

Keep It Real

I never stood for the pledge
I can't promise my allegiance
You shouldn't call yourself the greatest
You can't promise my freedom

Liberty and Justice for All?

Inspired by My Experience with Racial Profiling in La Crosse, WI

I pledge allegiance to the flag of the United States of America, and to the republic for which it stands, one nation under God, indivisible, with liberty and justice for all.

I wonder if they really meant those words when they wrote them, were they thinking about me? 'Cause I was the kid in the backyard of their mansion picking cotton all day. Not to mention my only nourishment consisted of cream and day-old biscuits served up in a pig trough. I'd be lucky to walk away with a full belly, all five of my brothers are hungry too. Mistakes do happen though, perhaps I slipped their minds.

Did they mean it when they counted three-fifths of my body as human? Something isn't right, it must be political jargon lost in translation, they see me for who I really am.

Ok, hold up, are you guys sure those two white men didn't murder Emmet Till? To me, it's clear as day that

it was a hate crime, so why did they walk away free?
I get locked up just for looking like the guy who did it.
Well, that was almost seventy years ago now, maybe
I should stop reading into it so much.

Officer, is it a crime to write in my journal on public
property? I understand I have a du rag on and look very
black at the moment, but can't you just leave me alone?
I swear I'm not devising a plan to break into these
white people's boathouses, I'm just trying to express my
emotions so they don't turn into rage. I don't want to be
another black incarceration statistic.

Is this country for or against me? I'm still not sure, but
it's been over an hour and the police cars still haven't
gone away.

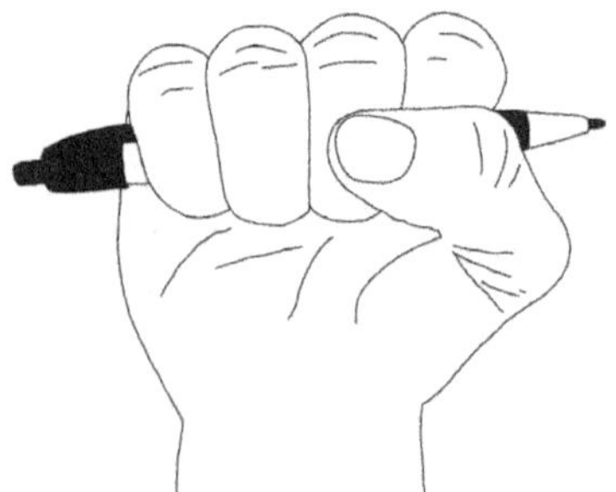

In George's Defense

I'm not saying all cops are bad
But I've found that some really are

On top of that
How can anyone police me
Without knowing about my scars?

Because they sure run deep
Back to the days
You weren't called the police

Your car was a horse
Pistol a rifle
You decided to keep the dogs

You chased me night and day
On my pursuit of freedom lane
I maintained a steady jog

Now all I ask of you
Is to see my pain
Because when I see you I'm reminded

Of all the times
Your "welfare checks"
Have left me broken, battered, and blinded

46

Ethnic Car Wash

Inspired by the US Educational System
I see a sea of young, black faces
Some are lost
Others are on their way
All of them believe that our minds are free today

Our building has a white name on the front
But serves all who look like us:
Dark skin
Power within

The price of freedom already paid
By our "long lost" kin
But no proof of purchase
The freedom bell doesn't ring

In class we are fed an American version of history
While the West African perspective
Typically remains a mystery

The reason is simple
The reason is plain
They don't want us to know the power
Behind our real last name

Because if we did our collective fate would change

And the power structures of today
Would be forced to rearrange

This is why they replaced Lumumba with Jackson
And Ude with Smith
A group of people without culture
Are easy to dismiss

The truth is that black history
Is the greatest story ever told
And is richer than mansa musa
With both hands full of gold

Our people are mighty
Our people are free
Our people run deep
Like the roots of a tree

So as I sit here and watch
The extent of this ethnic car wash
I make it obvious
That I am thoroughly displeased

Because what we call education
Is really indoctrination
And is responsible for infecting our children
With the American disease

Melanated Masterpiece

From the waves in your hair
To your beautiful broad nose
You ought to be cherished
Like a delicate rose

Your melanated skin
Which comes in many hues
Is such a wonder to the eye
That it's always on the news

You smile so bright
That it shines in the dark
The way you light up a room
Is a true work of art

You are beautiful, black child
I say this without a doubt
I hope with time you will see
What I'm talking about

Hoop Dreams

Inspired by My Basketball Career
As a young black child
My impression was mild
When I thought of being anything
But an athlete

I saw heroic black men
Win titles and awards
Battling on the court
For economic rewards

As I grew up I got better
And my handle got tight
I started getting buckets
In my hoop dreams at night

I was a driven young man
Who was looking for a way
To provide for my family
And cure our financial plague

So I woke up early before school
So I could practice my shot
And after class was over
I headed to work at the shop

When my shift was through
I went on to the gym
If I wanted to make the league
The margin for error was slim

This was my life
Every spare moment was spent dribbling a ball
Praying one day I'd get that glorious call

In high school I was the best
And averaged twenty-five points a game
So when I didn't get a scholarship
I didn't know what to blame

Am I too small?
Not quick enough?
Did I play for the wrong team?

Should I have worked harder?
Ate a better diet?
Should I give up on my dream?

I ended up at a school that was labeled D3
And in my heart I felt like I failed
A misled black kid who fell victim to hoop dreams
But in my darkest hour the truth prevailed

Every step of the way
I've been conditioned to say
One day I'll play in the NBA

But what they failed to say
In a peculiar way
Is there's only 450 roster spots to give away

With competition this fierce
The best guys make it to the top
While the rest of us get cut
And are labeled a flop

Having to start a new career from scratch
While our peers are well equipped
I wish someone had told me I stumbled and slipped

With that being said it's clear to see
This system appraises black worth
Based on our physicality
And will exploit my athletic qualities
But undervalue me

Cirque Du NBA

Come one come all!
It's time for a brawl!
A mighty negro showdown!

The Greek freak!
Is so unique!
He'll show your team a throwdown!

Keep your eyes on Steph!
He's sure to chef!
At least five 3's a game!

Don't miss the show!
Get on the road!
To watch the negros play their game!

The Center

Inspired by My Time at LCEC in Madison, WI

Sweep, sweep, sweep
That's the sound my broom makes as I sweep these
dusty halls.

*So long as we spend our money outside of our
community, is precisely how long we will be the victims
of economic enslavement.*
That's the sound of Malcolm X, enriching my
impressionable, African mind.

rattle-rattle-rattle-rattle, rattle-rattle-rattle-rattle, waaaaa
That's the sound of black people wheeling their weekly
ration of food from the pantry to their car. Oh yeah,
and a baby crying.

doon, doon, doon-doon-doon, swish! "In yo' face, nigga!!"
That's the sound of black young men playing pickup
ball after a long day of school.

"Yo Z, you're the janitor now? Hell nah, that could never be me!"

That's the sound of more black young men, playfully criticizing my current job title. To be completely honest, I didn't get the joke, and part of me doesn't want to. I fear that if I begin to perceive the black struggle in this nation as a joke, I'll laugh myself into ignorance and normalize our impoverished condition. So I'll take a page out of Malcolm's book and sit at this black table and not eat. Why? The food they give us is tainted, you see?

Pass the Okra Please!

Did you know the most malnourished ethnic group
In America
Are African Americans?

Did you know the most malnourished country
In the world
Is Haiti?

Did you also know that malnourished means
Malfunction of the body
Mind and spirit too?

Well now you know why we act the way we do
And maybe if you didn't receive proper nourishment
You would act this way too

40 Acres and a Lie

Inspired by My Travels to Baton Rouge, LA

I hop out of my van suited up for a good day's work. Steel toes are steelin', orange vest is blindin', and my grippy gloves are a perfect fit. I proudly walk into the new state-of-the-art Amazon warehouse and scan in with my ID tag. I head over to my assigned lane for the day and get to work. After the initial workman's high wears off, I find myself knees and elbows deep in the most repetitive work I've ever done in my life. The package drops down the shoot; I scan it with my scanner and place it on the pallet. Drop, scan, place. Drop, scan, place. "Hey, pallet man! This stack's all done, come wheel it out of the way for me." Drop, scan, place. I can't help but notice this rhythm sounds a lot like the one my ancestors used to vibe to back in the day, but that rhythm went a little something like this: Locate the cotton, pick it, and place it in the bag. Locate, pick, place. Locate, pick, place. "Hey, bag man! My bag is all full, come grab it so I can start with another one." Locate, pick, place. At this point, a depressive episode sinks into my head, and this poem comes to mind:

We were promised 40 acres and a mule
But were given 40 hours which make me weak
This shitty deal has left my mind sore

And body meek
Don't even ask about my future

If I had one worth mentioning I would surely speak up
The pain is reflected by the liquor in my cup
You would do the same

I take a look around
And observe my surroundings with fierce scrutiny
I see my brothers and sisters working labor jobs
Aching in distressed unity

It should come as no surprise
That I criticize this nation so brutally
It's clear that slavery has taken a different form

How have we grown so numb to this mistreatment
And in mistreating one another?
To fix this we must pretend we are all Gods undercover
If you ask me this is the last truth to be uncovered
Before the real change comes

'Cause we didn't come here to work our lives away
Breaking our back ten times over while they get paid
To sit there and sip their lemonade

This is a sick game

Embraced by those with an even sicker mind
Morally I find it quite difficult to find

Loopholes written within the rules so I can exploit
To fill my pockets and retire in the burbs of Detroit
Looking down on the plantation I created out of greed
That ain't what humanity needs

Give a little, take a little
I scratch your back and you scratch mine
Maybe then we can all sit back, have a beer, unwind
And turn this plantation into a gold mine

Poverty Trap

I give you 40 hours of my
Time
Energy
Attention
And care

And in return you give me
Stress
Anxiety
Depression
And just enough money to keep me there

Tools of the Trade

Inspired by My Travels to St. Louis, MO

Driving through the ghetto of St. Louis, I can't help but notice the skyline doesn't match my surroundings. These towers up ahead look so new and well kept, while the abandoned factories and schools around me look abused, run-down, and forgotten. It's at this moment that I realize we live in the shed, not even the backyard itself—the shed. You see, the shed is where you tuck away the things that are unpleasant to the eye but play far too big a role in your life to get rid of. With that being the case, our home reflects this negligent attitude. No one pays much attention to us, unless we're needed of course. And even then we're tossed around like emotionless objects of utility. This inhumane treatment makes sense because in the eyes of many we're unbreakable pieces of iron, nothing more than tools of the trade. This mistreatment has forged the rough exterior you see when we walk down the street, but it's only an illusion, a survival tactic, if you will. We're extremely delicate on the inside, but most people don't look close enough to see that. It's ignorance. But honestly, it's far worse than ignorance because you are quite aware of the concrete wasteland we come from. How could you not be? We bang around in this shed all day hoping for an upgrade in our position, and when our cries go unanswered, our delusional perspective leaves us no choice but to turn our anger against one another. In short, we're killing each other trying to get your full attention. By full I mean not just your eyes and ears but your heart. Your heart is what I'm truly interested in because once that connection is made, I'm free. Your heart wouldn't allow you to devalue my life to the extent that it has been. So until that day, in the shed I remain, awaiting the day you decide to see me as I am, which is not a tool of the trade, but a human being to be honored. And to be honest, I'm beginning to doubt that day will ever come.

Black Jesus

When you look at me
I know you see
A source of exploitation

Baggy jeans
And foolish talk
Of an equal nation

How do you know you're right?
What if I'm Jesus Christ?

Just a Kid from the Hood

Inspired by the Gun Violence Epidemic in Black America
The first thing I do in the morning
Is put on my mask
Where I'm from you can't leave home without it
Like an alcoholic with a flask

Over the years my mask has turned into a uniform
I'm suited up head to toe
In case anyone wants to try me
I'm ready to go

Retro 3's on my feet
Tucked in my belt is the heat
Baseball cap on my head
Gotta be red

I got the pack in my backpack
'Cause my daughter has to eat
Head on a swivel as I step out the door
Gotta be discreet

Is this the life I chose?
Or did it choose me?
Either way I'mma keep it pushin'
'Cause I'm in too deep

My teachers always told me
I'm too smart for the streets
But school was never my thing
I found my home in the jungle of concrete

Besides
Why break your back in construction
When you can hustle and rob?
I make more money like this
Than with a regular job

There's a risk to this life
But risk is all that I know
When you come from my city
They don't want you to grow
So you gotta hustle and get you some dough

But I won't lie
This street life is getting to my head
It's hard to be comfortable
When the ops want you dead

I almost got caught up last week
On a deal that I made
They tried to rob me of a pack
But I wasn't afraid

I probably should've been
But people around me are dying every day
So I live with the heat
Like my name is Dwayne Wade
In case anybody wants a fade

I look my daughter in the eyes
And I'm ashamed to say
I don't want her to end up with a man
Like me one day

She deserves someone better
Who writes sweet letters
And has a level head on his shoulders

I hope I'm here to see her grow older

Stress Bomb

I'm a ticking time bomb
Strategically placed
Next to the ones I love

Sit in the back
Be tight, don't lack
Are you even a man at all?

You push my buttons
Until I explode
Next to the ones I love

Collateral Damage

My dad is always in and out of the house. I wonder
why he doesn't just choose one? Whenever I did that
Grandma would tell me I'm either in or out, and
I better pick one quick. I wish she was here to tell
Daddy that. When Daddy comes home I always run to
give him a big hug. I like the way he smells like flowers
after he's been away. I ask Mommy where he goes at
night when he's not at home, she says he's at work.
One time, Daddy stayed at work for a whole year! I was
really sad when that happened; the only way I could
talk to him was on the phone or through a TV screen.
It was good to see him, but I couldn't smell the roses
or feel his big, warm hug. I don't think I like work that
much; when I grow up, I'm going to work from home.

Gunshot Lullabies

Inspired by My Travels to Baton Rouge, LA

I lay my head on the pillow
Pop pop pop!
Blood on the leaves of a weeping willow
Pop pop pop!
I hope they didn't aim at all
Pop pop pop!
I hope a black body didn't fall
Pop pop pop!

I can already hear Momma crying
And children dying
On the inside 'cause their daddies gone

How can I look that child in the face
And explain their father isn't a disgrace
He's just a product of his environment

How can I look that child in the face
And explain they must change the future of our race
Otherwise their children will have to face
The pain of loss the same as them

I lay my head on the pillow
Pop pop pop!
Blood on the leaves of a weeping willow

Pop pop pop!
I hope they didn't aim at all
Pop pop pop!
I hope a black body didn't fall
Pop pop pop!

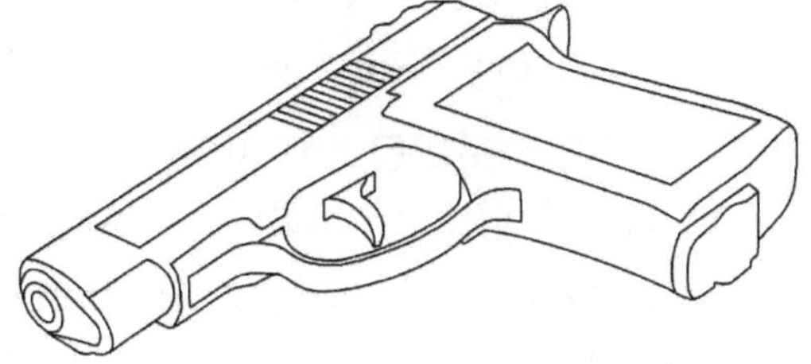

Damn That Man Willie Lynch

Inspired by the Willie Lynch Letter

It seems that after 400+ years of abuse and degradation, we have internalized this outrageous behavior and begun to inflict it upon one another. Instead of massa beating our children into obedience, we decided it would be less painful if we inflicted the blows. Instead of white society calling us niggers and bitches, we determined that black lips would neutralize the sting. And lastly, instead of slave catchers and lynch mobs murdering our people in cold blood, we have taken it upon ourselves to pull the trigger. This destructive behavior has become so widespread in our community that it's often accepted as "black culture." When in reality, our subculture of violence is the manifestation of the seeds of turmoil that were planted within our minds during the days of slavery. These seeds were planted with the intention of tainting our familial soil, leaving our offspring infected with an inclination of inferiority, a predisposition to false pride, and a demeanor of desperation. When harvested, this strange fruit achieves massa's ultimate goal of ensuring dependence on his system, through the annihilation of our own.

Why the Long Face?

Just an angry black man
Who's angry at the world
For unspeakable transgressions
That'll make your toes curl

Lemme' tell you why I'm so angry
Why my face is so long
I'll tell you all the ways
This world has done wrong

When I go to school
I don't learn what you do
I'm taught to survive
Not thrive like you do

When I walk down the street
In the suburb or hood
My skin raises questions
And none of them good

I'm traumatized still
From my roots in this nation
Yet I'm treated like a dog
Begging for donations

The God you gave me is whack

He doesn't look like me
When I practice my Voodoo
You call it blasphemy

I exclaim my life matters
And protests break out
Why can't you guys see
What I'm talking about

One more for the road
Maybe this will stick in your head
When I express my anger
I end up dead

Yes, I'm an angry black man
You should be angry too
If you can't find a reason
Imagine a mile in my shoes

www.ingramcontent.com/pod-product-compliance
Lightning Source LLC
Chambersburg PA
CBHW061431050726
47593CB00006B/2312